Fabio Morábito

TOOLBOX

Translated from the Spanish by Geoff Hargreaves

Illustrated by Bernard Recamier

Text first published in the USA in 1995 by Xenos Books

This edition first published in 1999 by
Bloomsbury Publishing, New York and London

Copyright ©1995 by Fabio Morábito

The moral right of the author has been asserted

A CIP catalogue record for this book is available from the British Library

ISBN 0 7475 4744 0

10 9 8 7 6 5 4 3 2 1

Text and cover design by NOTICE 51
Printed in the United States of America by
R.R. Donnelley & Sons Company, Harrisonburg, Virginia

CONTENTS

PREFACE

Paul Eluard's well-known remark, "There are other worlds, but they're all in this one," is actually a borrowing from a tradition that supposed the co-existence and simultaneity of different planes of creation, of worlds that we cannot ordinarily discern, but with which we can make some sort of contact. That tradition is occultism. The plurality of worlds isn't the only acknowledged debt that the Surrealists owed to the occult. Another is automatic writing, a practice common in the nineteenth century, before the discovery of the unconscious, among occultists bent on catching glimpses of alternative worlds, and a method of writing which, by interlacing irreconcilable elements, bears witness to the unity of all things. Surrealism transformed these borrowings and bequeathed them to us in the context of an expanding universe. Today, when in both painting and literature the communicable and the incommunicable, as André Breton used to say, have ceased to be contradictory, the number of worlds open for exploration has grown s i g n i f i c a n t l y . Gaining access to the different worlds that are interwoven with our quotidian one is an enterprise dear to the imagination at its most elemental. Niels Bohr's model of the atom still excites in children a dream of numberless solar systems akin to our own, where the earth is seen as a small particle in a larger system, which in its turn is part of a still larger one, which in its own turn is part of a still larger one, and so on *ad infinitum*. The unity of the microcosm and the macrocosm is reflected, of course, in fractal theory and its computer generated images, which bestow a morphological unity on a universe of parallel worlds into which mankind can sink itself. Behind this fascination with the unity of traversable worlds stands the idea of cosmogony, an idea that refused to be eclipsed by versions of creation from religion and astrophysics. The formation of a universe ought to imply the co-existence of planes, that infinitude of parallel worlds. The imagination is then faced with the challenge of thinking out novel worlds adjacent to our own, unsuspected worlds with their own logic, that is to say, their own physical laws, worlds possible, worlds improbable, worlds unimaginable. Literature is a fertile filed for these permutations. The recent great designers of alternative worlds, such as Jorge Luis Borges, Italo Calvino, J.R.R. Tolkien, and Shushaku Endo, play games with cosmogony beyond the strict needs of poetic creation. When Fabio Morábito selects for his title page John Cage's phrase "Start from scratch," he follows in their footsteps. The reader should be ready to participate in the formation of a possible world, now accessible for the first time. The "scratch" (or "zero" in the Spanish translation) to which Cage's phrase makes reference (in his book, *A Year from Monday*) is not nothingness; zero is a number which, although it lacks value, encodes all numeration, the point of departure and the possibility of order. It can't be an accident that tools--indispensable objects for making humans truly human--are the agents of this new permutation. Tools demonstrate an otherness right here in our own world; they are the first thrust toward the machine, toward what, in the end, must have a life independent of its creator. That fragmentary cosmogony of instruments conceived as autonomous things is what this book is. It gives shape not to a metaphysic, nor to a narrative of the world's creation, but to a poetic phenomenology in which things are objects not simply thought out but endowed with qualities as well. Here it is worth recalling Anaxagoras, the philosopher who twice started from scratch. He was the first to postulate that mankind possessed greater intelligence by virtue of its hands, and also the first to conceive a universe composed of indivisible units of different sizes, some bigger, some smaller. In Toolbox Morábito would appear to take literally the founding principle of Anaxagorean cosmogony, according to which all things were joined as one before the intellect--itself a thing, but of the purest sort--set them in order. This original, primitive fusion of everything implies, in pre-Socratic thought, that within every object of the universe there exists a portion of every other object; in other words, everything interpenetrates everything else. Aristotle declared this theory indefensible; according to his metaphysic, everything pre-existed in separate form. Nevertheless, he valued, surprisingly, the imaginative element in Anaxagoras' cosmogony. "Although the proposition that in the beginning everything was mixed together is nonsense, yet, if we follow it to its conclusion and articulate it, we may end up with a language rich in novelties." A language not founded in truth, but itself a mixed bag. Such a language, which in fact supposes that "there is a part of everything in everything" and which at the same time

"starts from scratch" and thereby detaches itself from all previous positive truths, is the wonder of Fabio Morábito's homemade, do-it-yourself cosmogony, inasmuch as ethical, physical, geometrical, spiritual, physiological, logical and psychological considerations, as well as technical, biological, rhetorical, anthropological, arithmetical, medical, geographical, existential and many other ones, co-exist on the same plane and within easy reach of each other, thanks to these irreconcilable elements switching places, reunited to give shape and movement to another possible world, which, as Eluard required, does exist in this one of ours. According to the Greek myth, Prometheus instructed mankind in the use of tools. In response there arrived a box which the gods handed over to Pandora to pass on to Prometheus. It ought to have remained shut, far beyond the reach of creatures who were just then mastering the use of fire, because inside it lurked all the evils associated with technology. Tools had their criminal side. When we recall Pandora's box, we remember also that at the bottom, after all the evils were set loose, there remained, but only just, the figure of Hope. When you open the *Toolbox* of Fabio Morábito, you'll find astonishing evidence that Hope is still in there and that, in return, technology keeps alive the flame of poetry's fire.

Jaime Moreno Villarreal

Start from scratch

JOHN CAGE

FILE & SANDPAPER

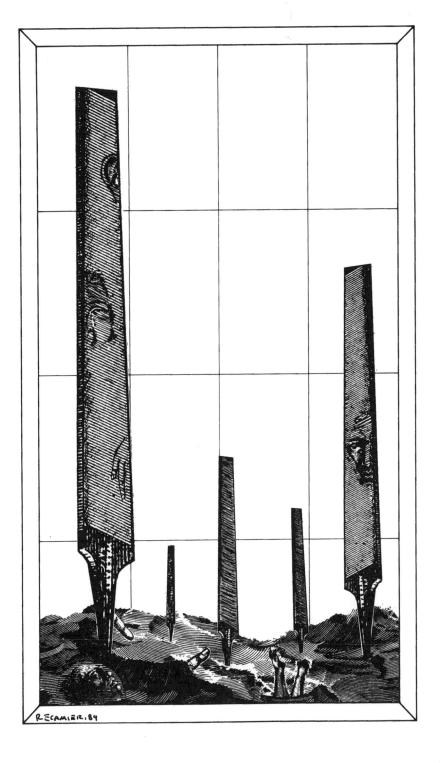

R.ECAMIER.89

The file is a blood relative of beheading instruments, cousin to the guillotine, kin to instruments that raze, amputate and cleave in half. But unlike the ice pick, the chisel or the machete, all of which concentrate their energies on a single point, the file spreads its impact over a network of points, an impact of apparent modesty and minimal caprices that a backward glance exposes as inexorable. A file works by persuasion; it reduces the force of its assault instead of intensifying it. In place of one strong jab, it resorts to a host of weak prods, one after the other, which attack in an orderly fashion like an army of ants, with more monotony than passion, but with no chance of a mistake. In its movements we can spy the action of waves as they crash deafeningly on the beach. Any projection that has to be eliminated from the surface of an object will suffer under the sea-like assault of the file. It will never have time to recover from a blow, because the blows that follow will already be coming down on it, submerging it. This is what a file does; it submerges whatever protrudes, anything that is over and above, it drowns it out thanks to the perseverance of its serried troops. That impression of massive numbers is so acute that at first glance it seems that a file is boiling. And this isn't to be wondered at. It is a tool stuffed with fire. Its livelihood depends on swearing oaths of loyalty. This characteristic need to swear oaths derives from the reticular design of its grating surface. A file is a succession of nodules. That's what those oaths are, its nodules. We already know only too well how those bumps squash the world into shape. "I swear I'll never love anybody but you," is the thing lovers tell each other, and their world is reduced to the room they currently occupy. That's what a file is like: it is pure narrowness, accumulation, asphyxia. Its grooves cluster into a labyrinth. Anything that gets bunched up too tight turns wrinkly; it becomes a file. There's a second reason a file swears oaths: it is blind. It has a thousand eyes, and that's what turns it blind, the way its thousand mouths render it mute. They swear away to the point of exhaustion. It's enough to glimpse at a file in action, to observe how it soldiers on and on, getting hotter and hotter, to know it never quits muttering its oaths and vows. It never leaves off spitting out a drizzle of chips, sawdust, splinters, or granules, exactly the way certain groups of men do when they swear, spitting on the ground to rid the body of its moisture, striving to become fiery and dry. A guy with water inside him is hardly one to be trusted. Water masks, it muddies, it effeminizes. A man who wants people to believe him when he takes a vow has to spit first and get tense and in order to confer tension and orneriness on his words. A file's the same. It has everything spitten out of it, its throat gets bone-dry, it is all scar and cauterizing flame. You can't touch it after it's been used. The grooves are so hot they're almost buzzing. They have been swearing away like women possessed. A file moves in when the other beheading tools can't get the foothold they need to do the job. It makes its appearance when the bump you want eliminated is too modest to merit a frontal attack, because files specialize in oblique offensives. A file gets cracking when its amputating kindred begin to slip and slide for want of a firm place to grip onto, when they lose their footing and start to look frivolous. A file never drifts off topic; it's a model of earnestness. It is incapable of being distracted. It is the diametrical opposite of oil and dampness.

A culture without files is threatened by esoteric and erotic dangers, by slither and skid; it's a culture where everything's come close to rolling away and skipping about, of taking wing, of blasting to smithereens the decencies of proportion and distance. In contrast, a file doesn't permit itself the slightest lapse, the most minimal break in its concentration. It suffices just to see how it functions to know that. Two opposing forces are exercised on it: one presses down on the surface you want filed and makes the file stick like glue to it, as if it wanted to reduce the file to immobility; the other, a longitudinal thrust, drives the file forward and represents that portion of the file's material that hasn't forgotten the pleasure of sliding along and that makes a constant effort to ensure that something happens. Out of this conflict arises the file, with its network of points, its crisscrossed ridges. There the primordial, urbane smoothness, which is a thing of water and loquaciousness, gets disciplined into a sort of virility, while the rustic interior, a thing of stone and gruff taciturnity, gets transformed into something slenderer and more docile that allows the speech to speak, the song to sing. The result is the file's perfect pronunciation—clear, rigorous, virtually human. A file speaks by using every one of its teeth, without swallowing a single vowel or consonant, doing justice to the whole alphabet, a paragon of good diction. Human beings who are subject to the same conflicting pressures, from the urbane and the rustic, from water and stone, are nothing other than files, ridged and wrinkled animals. That's why they possess the gift of speech. Unlike the file, sandpaper isn't constituted of grooves but of a horde of granules which sweeten its impact. Here, instead of a job of persuasion, we get what we might call the work of prayer, even of supplication. What must have inspired the invention of sandpaper, as well of the file itself, is the beach. The sea keeps itself clean by rubbing itself on beaches, and in return, as a poet put it, it puts the beaches to sleep. But beaches not only polish and cleanse; they also soak up water and get sodden. The file with its grooves easily gets rid of any liquid; it's a perfect example of a drainage system. Sandpaper, however, is pure pulverization. This makes it more flexible and able to sneak into corners impossible for a file, but it brings it closer to chaos and dampness. But both of them, file and sandpaper alike, whether they are dry or moist, swearing oaths or abjectly begging, get the same type of pleasure: that of abrasion, erosion, abstraction. Thanks to them, all materials can, with a bit of patience, get to the bottom of their true nature, can reach their innermost noontide.

SPONGE

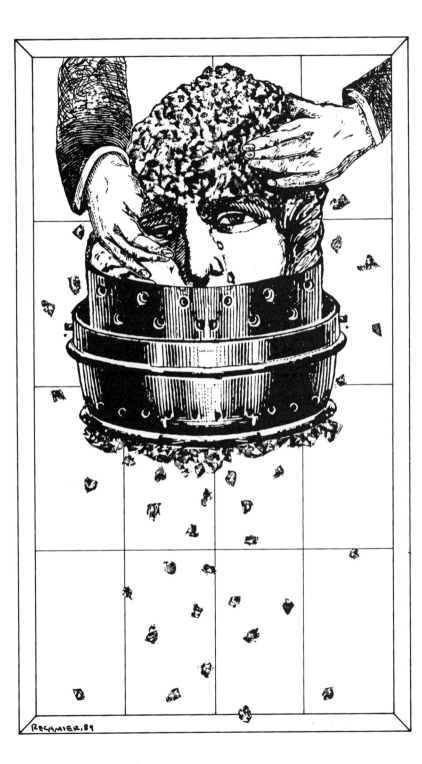

RECAMIER, 89

If we place across a level surface a certain number of passageways and galleries which crisscross and communicate, we end up with a labyrinth. If we then connect up to this labyrinth from all directions—upwards, downwards, sideways—still more labyrinths, that is to say, other levels of passageways and galleries, we end up with a sponge. A sponge is the apotheosis of the labyrinth, but what is linear and stylized in a labyrinth becomes, in a sponge, uncontrolled and chaotic. The material in a sponge gallops outwards, rejecting any notion of a center. It is pure dispersion. Let's imagine a herd of animals fleeing from the assault of a feline predator, and inside this herd a group of individuals situated at a fair distance from the predator, but no less terrified because of that. This section of the herd, marginal but not peripheral, fraught with terror but relatively safe, is a sponge, a blend of delirium and invulnerability. It is this blend that makes us feel that, of all our tools, the sponge is the least in control of itself, the most outward-looking, totally prodigal, wholly bent on nirvana. Its thousands of cavities and galleries are like the disintegration that precedes the final pulverization in all explosions. Its astonishing lack of weight is already a first step toward collapse and absence. In contrast, the lightness of a bird's feather has little merit; it is too closely bound to its smallness; it is a lightness that manifests itself without surprises. But a sponge's lightness, on the other hand, is something heroic. This lightness is proof of its total application and dedication, a dedication so extreme that it begins to look like an insatiable rapacity. A sponge sucks up and absorbs but has no receptacle outside itself to hold what it absorbs. It has no digestive system. It doesn't process anything, it doesn't retain anything, it doesn't establish property rights over anything. All it can do is lend itself out, right down to its very last bit of tunneled connections. But what's the point? The sponge itself doesn't know. That's why it never speaks, never tells tales. Water invades it like a buzzword nobody understands but which all the tunnels gabble over and over with an incendiary panic. Not a single mouth remains silent. The sponge is amoral. Hence the ease with which it is penetrated both above and below. Uncritically it lets you poke into its most intimate recesses and relieve it of all its secrets. All you need to do is to turn into water. And which of us doesn't do that, when we're confronted by a sponge? Let's consider a man who has a sponge in his hand, observing how he fondles it and peers at it. Despite himself, he is imitating the action of water. Water never finds itself in as much control of its expression, its voice, as when it's contained inside a sponge. Water's principal business—running down—discovers inside a sponge, in that concentrated, tangible setting, a perfect opportunity to perform all its tasks, to demonstrate its abilities in a laboratory setting, as it were. A sponge with its thousand branch lines manages to hold water in check, so that it may recognize its own nature, without difficulty, in a clean and human fashion. Inside a sponge water recaptures, fleetingly, its hands and feet, a trunk, fingers and toes, cartilage—in other words, a seed of self-awareness. It regains consciousness after it carries out the specific job of scrutinizing in depth, but without mistakes or lapses in attention, a body that was keeping itself dry. This is the plenitude of water, and also of love.

When all is said and done, there are few things in this world like a sponge. It is anonymity in its purest form. It has no character, that is to say, no habits, no fads, no self-indulgent lapses, no unfeeling moments, no bouts of hardheartedness. The key to its nature is its equanimity. There are no roadblocks in it; nor are there expressways, shortcuts or escape routes. Each membrane and cartilage participates in the common task with equal intensity. It's as if the material, once and for all, had refused to accumulate force at any one point, or the smallest build-up of reserve energy—as if it had made a personal vow to dissipate even the slightest hint of ganglion, thew or sinew—as if through its tortuous reckonings, detours, comings, goings, endless recomings and regoings, it had put an end to all fattiness, inertia and stubbornness, to every stupidity. The result: a material that is agile and wide awake, traversable and pronounceable. And something else: a powerless material, unknowing in the finest way, without being foreign to emotion. Half of a half of a half: here's the little law that controls a sponge, a law that a sponge obeys to the limit, with admirable determination and rigor, a law which means, to put it bluntly, breaking things down to the hundredth or thousandth part or to whatever fraction is necessary to neutralize any attempt to build up sediment, tribal feelings or patriarchal structures. Given that its passion is for dubious schemes and binges, for lubrication and pumping, what it requires is forking roads and detours, and detours within detours, branches of branches of branches—everything reduced to fractions, everything down to half of a half, everything changing direction, everything feminine, everything ready and waiting.

Hence its vocation as a filter, a distiller. The filter, as we all know, is a fall broken at the last moment, at a minute fraction from disaster, a tool of dissuasion; it dissuades by holding stuff back and making it dizzy. It is a cross-examination. Guilt, that permanently illicit bag of booty, remains at the end open to view and neutralized as a dollop of goo. What stays behind is the essence, the initial poverty, since a filter is nothing other than a journey back-to-front in search of a lost beginning. You could call it a reminder, maybe a confession. And yet, paradoxically, a sponge is the expression of a failing memory. It doesn't admit sums or accumulations. It's Franciscan. And another thing, it has an athletic disposition; it can't allow anything to get cold or grow old. So, although we may not want to, every time we squeeze a sponge in the cartilages and tendons of our hands, a secret desire is hinted at, one that never leaves us, a desire to re-invent ourselves from the bottom up, to be different, to be as accessible and light as we were on our first day. There's no shadow of a doubt that our first day was just that, a sponge.

OIL

RECAMIER, 89

Oil is water that has lost its get up and go, its cheeky forward drive. Having exhausted all its routes, it's discovered treading over ground it trod before. It is water that has turned its back on the world. It is *de trop*. It has forfeited its old rights of way across the floor and now has to step to one side in favor of fluids younger and grander. It is luxury water, which after so much flowing has felt the weight of experience, maybe bitter experience. It's as if it had other water at its service; hence its sumptuousness, not far from prostration, for where there is sumptuousness, there's always somebody on his knees, tied with bonds. So oil is a form of water that needs to prop itself up on another form, one hand placed over another hand—that's the fundamental nature of oil—and this disability makes it uneasy. It's water clogged with sand, a water that went astray on a hairpin bend that cut down its progress and couldn't shake off the sand, so it said goodbye to foam and withdrew into itself, taciturn, choked with grit. It is water that is weak at the knees. Incapable of running, of instinctively shaking off hazards, of stepping warmly on every stone, of producing a crystal-clear diction, oil has turned snooty, calculating, sedentary. After it used up all its routes, it became reflexive. It ruminates and shilly-shallies like somebody who cautiously returns to his home ground and rather than walk further, occupies it, seizes possession. All possessive forces keep going over the same ground, and oil is back home again. It is water with a predatory air. While young waters disinterestedly investigate the earth, oils get on their high horse, develop ambitions. They are water on the up and up. Their sandiness lets them climb up things slowly but steadily. Without oils, in fact, our world would lack surprises, would be constantly heading downhill, tyrannized by gravity, a place of limitless flatness. In the long run a world without oil would become geometric. But oil puts a stop to that possibility by being anti-doctrinaire. It proves this by its cautious progress, its sounding things out. It is water with its hopes shattered. It forms around objects a zone of confusion that saves them from being brutally scrubbed by the world. It encloses them in a hypnotic state. That's how lubrication works. Any piece that is lubricated subtly washes its hands of other pieces, it achieves autonomy, and within the mechanism as a whole, it recaptures the rhythms of its own individual will, or at least the illusion of them. Oil really does project an individual temperament; it comprehends and knows how to listen. Hence where water, distracted and gullible, charges ahead, oil turns back, full of guile, and holds itself in check and takes in its surroundings. It neither tosses things away nor draws conclusions. Instead, it discerningly imprints a face and an age on whatever it touches. Everything oily has a name. Without oil there would be no culture, no commerce, no transportation. Oil is water with a burden to carry. Thanks to oil, our world has different hues, and things swap postures and places, and open themselves up to unsuspected uses. Oil, if we may put it this way, acts like a butler; it's the bridge or the mattress which make affable contact possible between things. It legitimates relationships and bestows a lasting stamp on them. It doesn't throw its weight around; it applies pressure with finesse, gets chatty, reanimates, civilizes. Deprived of oil, we'd be subject to water's monastic lifestyle and forever uncouth. Kinkiness and hope would be tabooed.

We'd live without cunning, but also without grace. Water searches for channels and always finds them. It loves order and repetition. Oil, which travels at one or two gears lower than water, has a multitude of eyes and that induces it to spill over and not exclude. It has lots of community spirit and is inventive. Where water settles disputes and gives each his own, oil jumbles things up in a utopian fashion. Every jumble contains a trace of utopia and puts rumors and spirited efforts to the test. It is a circus strongman. Its job involves rigmarole. The oil that covers over a certain material, that lubricates it—a pipe or whatever—is subtly duplicating it, like an echo. It extends it microscopically in order to take away its claws and to help it relax. Oiled materials collide with no more than a shrug. The curtain of oil functions like an evangelizing fire and individual points of friction lose their gleaming sharpness. A sense of overall enthusiasm prevails, for oil is like the pump that vitalizes the whole contraption, getting the parts to pass from a state of sleepiness to excitement, and then to humility, setting aside their private concerns the more they pitch in on the main job, whose whole point is mutual contact. Oil, therefore, is the speediest of messengers, leaving nobody uninformed or confused. Its masterpiece, or rather its whole *raison d'etre*, is hugging things, mixing them together, cooking them, rounding them out to perfection. Unlike water which heads toward the sea, oil takes any route it can to produce a stew, a sense of communion.

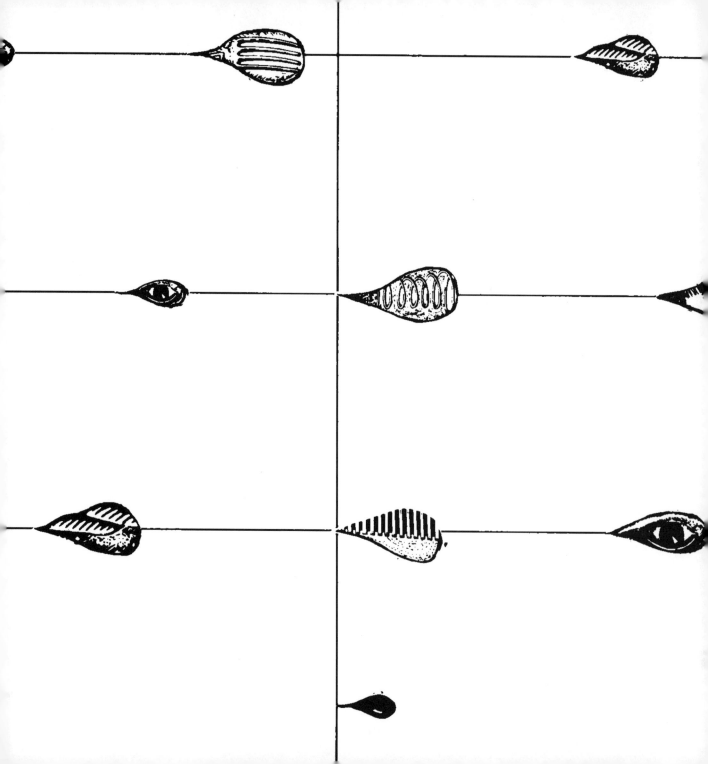

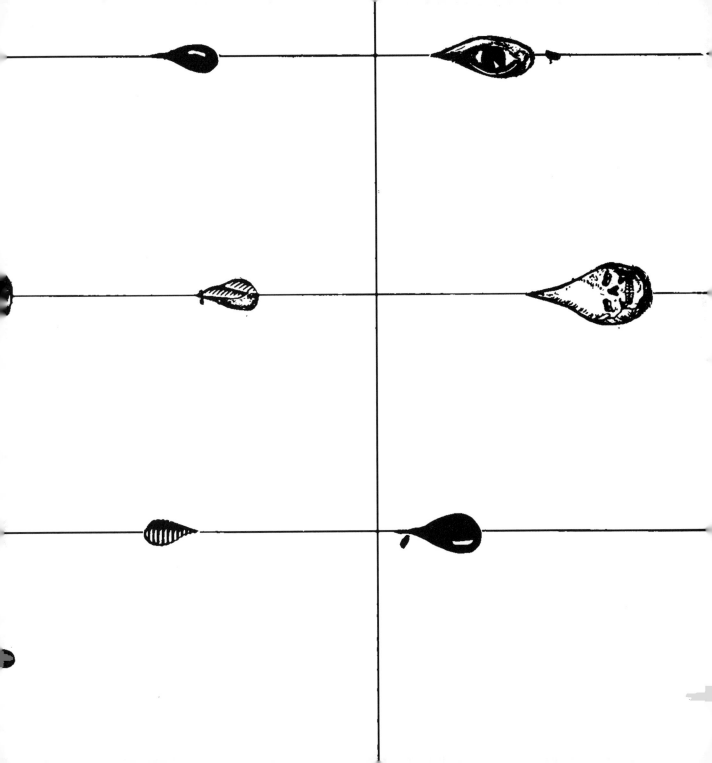

PIPE

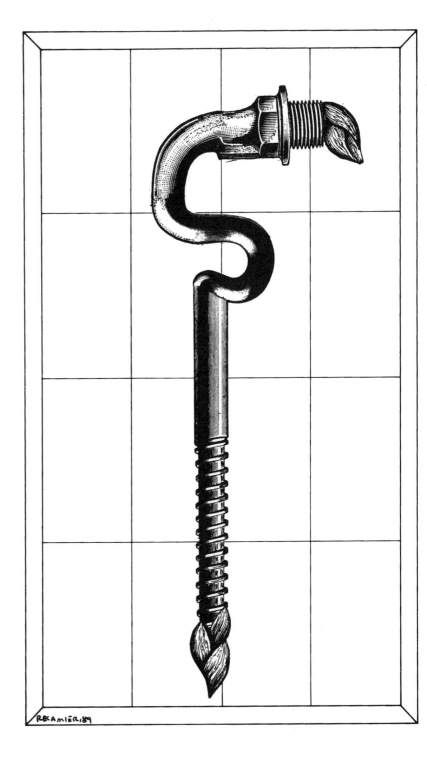

RECAMIER, 89

The job of a pipe is to answer the call of duty, to uphold its honor and to hold in its breath. At the point where we take a second breath, where we burst into a cackle of laughter or cross the boundary of the absurd, that's where there's an end to piping. Other tools mask their objectives well, but not so a pipe. Moreover, a pipe doesn't even have an objective to hide, it produces no product, it's the biggest layabout in the toolbox—and the least likely to accept graft. For all its mildness, it's the tool with the best luck, because what goes through a pipe is always a novelty. A pipe's chock-a-block with the spirit of Sunday, Sunday being our weekly serving of smoothness. On Sundays the force of gravity takes a seat, and we are firmer on our feet. And the more level our stance, the more we turn into statues. Pipes are selected slices of smoothness, they are fillets of level being.

To be present on the inside of a pipe is an honor. It's like travelling on a public mission. Everything about a pipe is well-appointed and well-mannered. Hence where the soil is not sufficiently obliging, one lays a pipe. A pipe means pressure. Whatever passes through a pipe acquires a note of urgency. You require something? Something absolutely must reach its destination? And without delay? Then a pipe is called for! If the expression "call for" didn't exist, then neither would pipes. "Hey you!" somebody shouts, cupping his hands round his mouth in the shape of a pipe, a rounded-out smoothness, as if a transfer from one world to another were desired, with a shout hooking them speedily together. Exactly! A pipe suppresses the world, it's a shortcut. Every shortcut is an act of flying, and pipes fly. Even under the soil they fly. They represent rootlessness, the international spirit, the triumph of the generic and of smoothness in things, because anything a tube carries inside itself is always unclear and official and is the smooth property of the nation.

A pipe is forever turning its back on us, telling us that we don't see the point, and, honestly, at what section of a pipe are we capable of even a superficial understanding, given that it is all a matter of oratory and flight? A pipe—and this is the plain truth—both is there and is not there. It belongs to others, it comes from a distance and goes off into the distance; it is all neck and backbone, nothing but the footsteps of the blind or the deaf-and-dumb. In short, a pipe is unreal, or at least somnambulistic. It hasn't a trace of irony or jocularity. It is corps-like, a quality that helps it surmount dents and bumps, to overcome tribal and ancestral resentments. It is smoothness in action. Pipes are the speech-form of the new generation and lubricants of the world; they heal old wounds and function by stretching themselves out. Where a bubble of violent force pops up, deaf to reason and writhing with trauma, pipes calm it down and lend it a voice, giving it length, allowing it space in the world, offering it a promise. They are great relaxers. Bestow smoothness on the savage, and you get docility: this is the motto of a pipe. Hence a pipe is a narcotic. There'd be no drugs without pipes. Every drug test out its piping on us and every hallucinogenic experience is comparable to the liveliness and disorderliness that flowing down a pipe produces. A pipe takes away strain and muddles things up, reestablishing the hasty outpouring of the earliest times, when things were easy because there were so few of them. So where you've got a pipe, you've also got not merely pressure, but a dazzling summary, for a pipe goes straight to the point; it's as if we were coursing over a stretch of ground well known to us, as if we were to say, "This section belongs to us, we have trodden it over and over countless times, and we know it all so thoroughly that by now we're totally within our rights to lay a pipe here." A pipe, in short, sums up the footsteps and glances that we employed in taking control of a stretch of rough ground, as if, by dint of stepping on it and gazing at it, we have brought out a polish in it. A pipe is an emblem of dominion fully   achieved.   It's   a   reward. That's why pipes always betray property owners. Where there are pipes, there has been penury and worried glances toward tomorrow. A man who possesses some form of ducting is one who, so to speak, sees and reaches out farther than others, who recognizes that he will endure, subtly, to the last. The hollow shape of a pipe indicates the will to organize oneself and endure. Its capacity for amplification, lamentation and violent expulsion is due to this very same asceticism. Just look at what the tube in a telescope or microscope can do. It recruits waves of light, isolates them, strips off their outer layers, cleans off their greasy worldliness, leaves them in a mystic state, for all to see, in a condition of perfect attention, of smoothness. Amplification is a peeling away, a modest explosion. Unfortunately, it's a short step from here to disemboweling as such, to the genuine explosion (think about canons, mortars, bazookas, even a simple blowpipe), and it's then that we'd like the pipe to be less even-tempered and more susceptible to bribery, with leaks everywhere, and specifically for the good of humanity, less straight and s   t   u   b   b   o   r   n   .

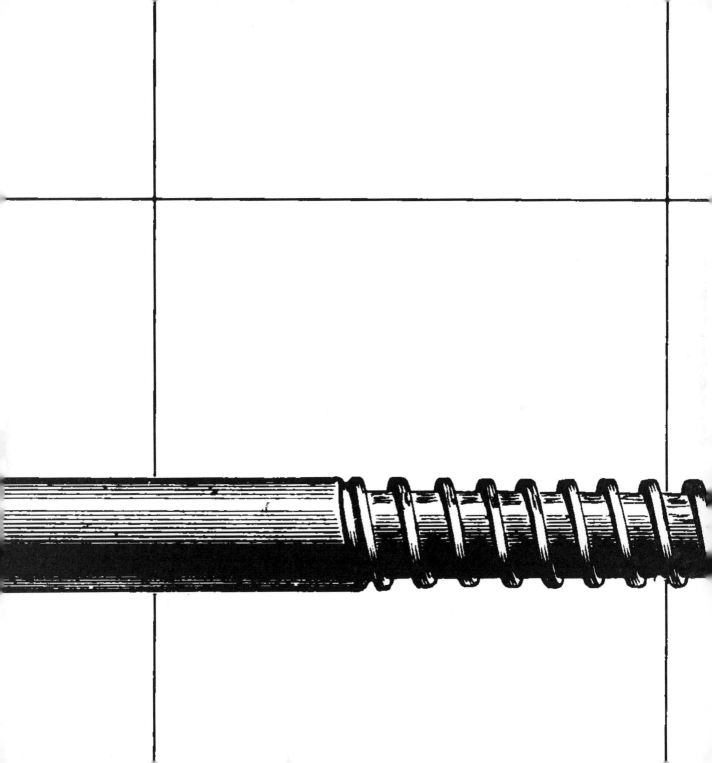

KNIFE

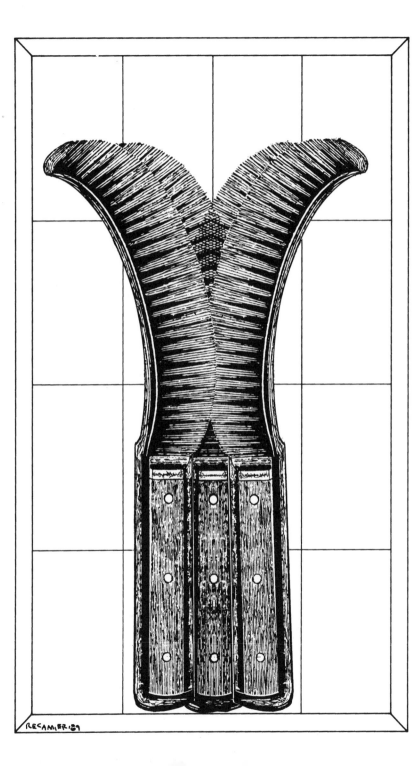

RECAMIER·89

A knife is an end point plus a sensation of cold. It settles accounts. It disheartens and sends into exile. Never ever, for any reason, does it glance backwards. Its whole being is forward motion, and yet it doesn't explore, investigate, make progress or learn things. It's an interjection! Why are other things so different from knives? Because at some moment, even if it's only casually, momentarily, other things double back, twist around, take a fancy to something and forfeit a fraction of time. This brief moment is enough to allow the approach of a turned back, a shadow, a stoutness of body and a chance to become something. And that's enough to put an end to a knife, the pure knife point. (What's known as the blade is simply a carousel of such points.) The point of a knife is radically void of memory and of bonds, it knows nothing at all, it is indebted to no one for anything, it casts no shadow. In a certain sense it is dead, it is a ruination, a cyst. It is what remains at the end, a thing that scorches, an ineluctable force, an enemy of skin and of reason—the skin and reason that do their jobs by wavelike motion, by absolution, by collective effort. A knife point is pure discord. It is the end result of a grievous distillation. Behind each point stand thousands of years. Its ability to wound comes from the enormous weight that, crouched on all fours, bruised and disciplined, is encased in it. The logic behind every sharpened object consists in arranging a situation in which one, pushed by many, gets its filthy and goes berserk on behalf of all. It's as if they all ran forward toward a point and then, suddenly, at a given signal, they went into reverse. There will always be somebody who is last to get into line; and this is the one who, to be frank, is prevented from getting into line. That somebody is the knife point, the sacrificial victim. The others thrust it away, so that it doesn't get mixed up with them; they treat it like a stinking pariah. The victim, in short, is the one whom the others push away, the one who has no fun. Every push he receives sets him farther from the tribe. Hence the gradualness with which things get sharpened to a point. It takes a lot of pushing for a victim to be finally transformed into the victim, for him to stand there all alone and accused in the face of the tribe, for him to reach the point of never again being assimilable. It's as if the tribe were painfully evacuating its bowels. To make the point clear, imagine a group of men clambering down a slope. Before long one of those at the rear hangs back and dodges behind a tree. Then another hangs back and dodges behind a boulder, then another behind a bush. Those up at the front aren't aware of this and carry on downhill; but the desertions continue. All of them, as soon as they sense they are dawdling slightly, take advantage of any chance feature of the landscape to find a hiding place. Until only one of the men remains on his feet, with no place to hide, stuck out in broad daylight. He turns back, but he can't see anybody. They've left him all alone. He is exposed. He is the knife point. And he can't scurry to cover back up the slope, because all the hiding-places are now occupied. He is the fall-guy, the excrement. This ironlike gradualness, this crafty advancing, constitutes the essence of a knife. Just look at the hardness and stubbornness of its blade. It is a brotherhood of the deaf. Nobody knows anything, nobody hears anything. They all push because they are pushed by others who are, in their turn, pushed by others. Nobody wants to be the last one left on the downhill trip, so they all push to get somebody ahead of them, and thanks to their pushing the closer they get to the abyss, the more brutal they become, until the last one turns into the knife point. They all ought to go home and forget the whole business, but in order to do that they'd have to climb back up the slope—which would take some doing. They prefer to see the business finished, to run a bit of a risk and stay to see who ends up exposed as the knife point. They want a close-up view, to see him with their own eyes. They need personal proof that the game has been played out, that the victim is somebody else and not them. That's why they're so pushy. But what do they mean by "victim"? They realize too late in the day that they've been tricked. There is no victim. The victim is going to be delivered up right now, in his sleepwalking progress toward the fire. The victim is the one who gets too far ahead, the one who wants to check out things more than he should, the one who doesn't brake in time and stands out from the mass, who turns into an undesirable excrescence, the lousy piece of shit, the knife point. He, then, is the one who gets burnt, the one who immolates himself and in so doing enjoys that secret triumph, that mystic exaltation which in due time overtakes every victim. This blending of repulsion and desire, of advancing and retreating, this holding-back without ever actually stopping—a characteristic of those who descend slopes— determines the nature of knives and everything else sharpened to a point. The shape of a knife evokes the image of an impulse not checked in time and recalls a slippery world where things abruptly escape our control and achieve a dangerously

nasty autonomy. It's as if a troop of cavalry, after routing the enemy forces, were to insist on pursuing them out of sheer momentum (or an excess of gallantry) until they found themselves deep in hostile territory, surrounded and besieged on all sides. The pig-headed cavalry troop which demonstrates its exaggerated forward drive and its feeble braking capacity perfectly represents a knife's equivocal nature, its tendency to backfire, to spill blood without intending to, and it also explains, incidentally, quarrels, the sudden, treacherous stabbing, the sordid slashing with a blade, the drunken knifing, misery and flight.

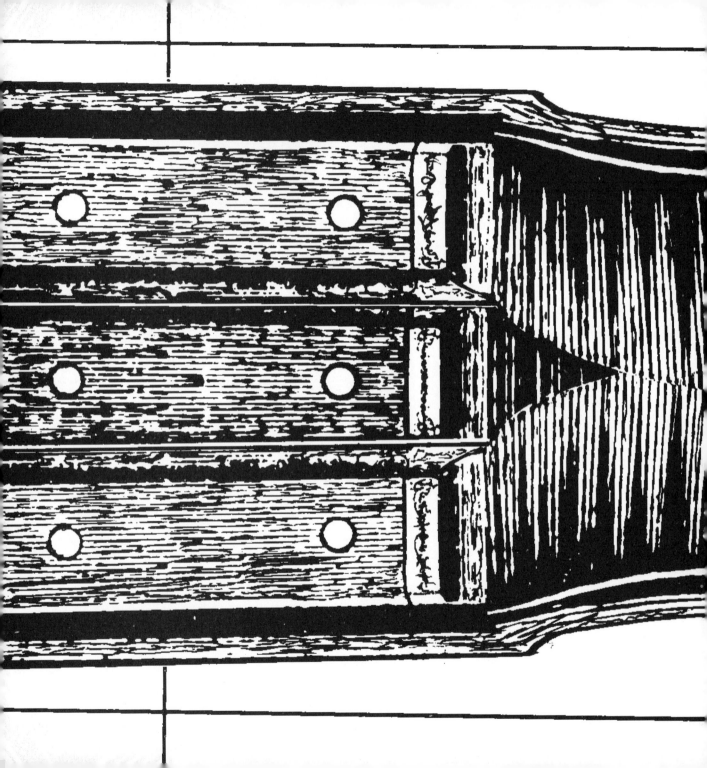

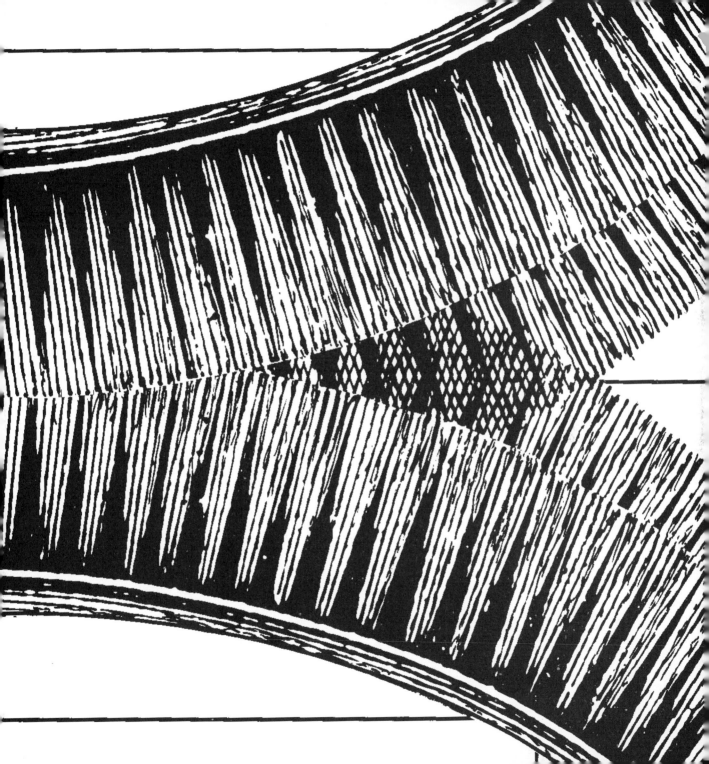

STRING

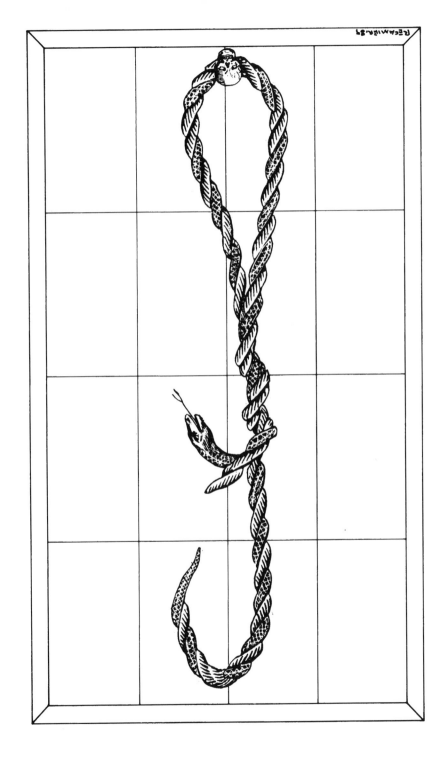

String is a dot elongated to the point of obsession, or to put it more precisely, it is a long succession of victims. Hence its passivity, its lack of faith in others, its overall apathy. String is a concatenation of the virtually dead, but mercifully, before actually dying, the poor creatures were ushered shoulder to shoulder into a compact group, the togetherness that constitutes string. At every second they expect, they almost seem to desire, the final hatchet-blow, the lightning flash of the descending guillotine. The total spinelessness of string makes it a closer relative of water than any other occupant of the toolbox. String can even give the impression of being water that is bound and gagged. Compared to water, which will countenance no other manipulation beyond being contained in a vessel, string seems to represent the possibility of a water that is more self-assertive, longer-lived, less transitory and more sedentary, a more palpable water, a Herculean water. But seen close up, it shows its real nature: it is a rosary of capitulations; at every point along a string there is tangible evidence of its prostration, its infinite melancholy; at every point someone throws in the towel and lets his arm be twisted. String is pure suffering. With too much body to be forever born again, the way water is, it still does not have the sturdy solemnness of bone. So every stimulus it receives acts as a profound mortification. Hence, perhaps, the spinelessness of string. The absence of a protective coating ought to be construed in this case as a defense, for it functions as an anesthetic. The various parts react separately; there is no common holocaust. String is vulnerable, perhaps excessively so, but it can't be beaten, flogged. Every bit of it has an individual life; there are no linkages, everything is an end-point, a last step on the staircase. So string, with difficulty, I grant you, is a total survivor. Hence its malleability, which brings to mind leftovers like ash, smoke, debris. String itself is a fire: a blaze of many blazes. This gives it its air of holiness. Holiness is the prerogative of the spineless. The first thing a saint renounces is his bones. Anyone who doesn't know how to renounce his bones may as well forget sainthood. Being a saint implies a withdrawal of effort, a debility without limits. As long as there is the least hint of internal supports or chassis, of even a minimum of coherence based on a supportive structure, or reinforcement, of balancing acts, holiness turns out to be a monstrous fraud. Blessed is he alone who never forgets to forget himself, even for a single second. String's like that, a convergence of acts of self-oblivion, and constitutes a concrete definition of that most difficult of renunciations, giving up breathing. Few things can equal string when it comes to holding one's breath and sinking into oneself. We could say that string is the hand we're always short of, that imaginary third hand, deeply devoted to us, which never lets us down or leaves evidence of its presence, a hand that has forsworn the desire to accumulate and hang onto things, simply so that it can extend the sense of life's translucence. And establish bonds. And offer good counsel. Anybody who goes back after an absence to the place where he lived and struggled constructively feels awkward in front of all the hands he left behind, the ties and knots, the reciprocities he made good. In short, his strings. Strings are always a wonder. They are the most spiritual of all the tools, the most deeply imbued with unconscious force. We've only got to watch people tightening or rolling up or loosening string to see why. A childlike excitement seizes them, because string is so easy, a sort of bread among the tools. Like bread, it often goes unnoticed. Like bread, it is one of the two mainstays of the settled life. String is the first step in the act of delegating. We give it a job to do, assign it a task. Leisure is possible only when all the strings are pulled tight and kept busy. What's a machine or an engine but a string ensemble? That's why it produces a vague unease to see a piece of string doing nothing, lying idle on the ground, the way a piece of bread on the floor unsettles us. Bread is never wasted, because there's always a mouth to feed. Likewise, string always has a service to offer. But that's not why string is so spiritual. Its spirituality derives from its vow of absolute poverty. There is nothing in string that refuses to go hungry. Its gastronomic ambitions are zero. This is because it moves like a relay race of fibers. Every exchange of the baton is an abdication of appetite and it's precisely these cleverly disjointed acts of fasting that make up a string. Thanks to the individuality of the threads, which hand over their separate bits of life with a forward, lunging movement, the string, like a mother, creates a continuity of hemp. A host of streams form one huge act of impatience; or if you like, a host of exhalations compose a single breath. In nothing else in the toolbox do we find an ongoing concordance quite like string for its marvelous blending of spirited elements. In fact, on that vegetable puff-pastry, on that vortex of threads and fibers which is string, it's almost impossible to let your glance rest easily, for string, once we examine it closely, is a multitude of strings. The truth of the matter is that string, what at any rate we call string, doesn't really exist, for who could grasp that lively bundle of bits and pieces? Could string itself even do it? Not unless it sprang into existence from nothingness in the very act of grabbing hold of itself. So who does control string long enough to stretch out its threads? Maybe God. Maybe the law of gravity. Or maybe, and most probably, it's just an illusion of our incurable pretensions to greatness.

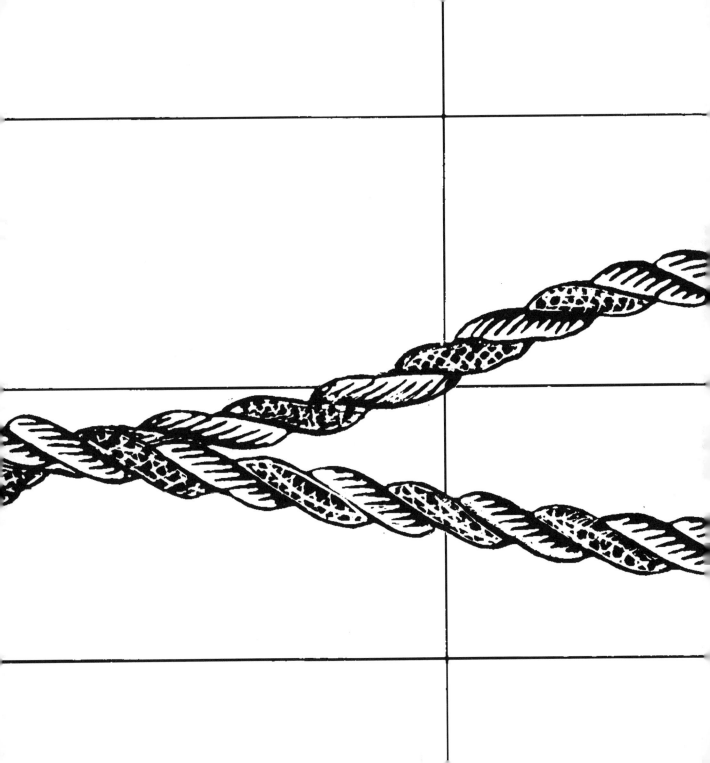

BAG

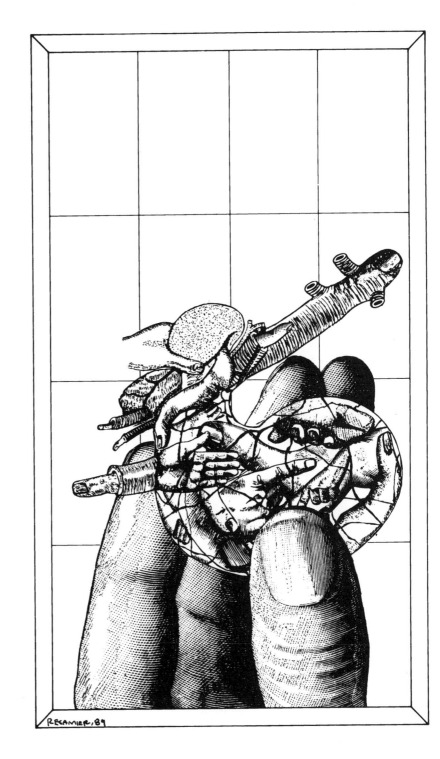

A bag is a juicy game for hands, for many hands, hands profoundly interlocked, so profoundly and liquidly implicated that no single one of them is capable of closing in on anything by itself or of exercising its legal rights over its own fingers.

A bag is a product of this struggle, of this pact, of this delicate sensibility and mutual forgiveness. Where there's a bag, there's brotherly love working co-operatively. And there's also extravagant waste, for the hands in a bag waste a lot of time. The shape of a bag is the shape of wasted time, of wasted energy. Every hand in a bag points at and flatters its buddies. They're all invited to the party, but nobody acts as host; they're all equally distinguished. A bag's merriment is the merriment of a space that has made light of its debts, of a celebration without an organizer, a court without a king. It is a merriment derived from a momentary loss of features. Like a laugh. A face that laughs wants to be another kind of face altogether; it cracks its features not because it would like to have different ones, but in order to have no features at all, to escape from them. A bag is the same. It runs away from its obligations, from knowledge, from experience. It shrugs off all sense of purpose. A bag is sediment, the last of the muscles, the lowliest of the tribe's guides. After the bag, bad weather sets in.

The hands of a bag trust each other, or they're scared of each other, because in the center of the bag there's a pearl that nobody dares lay a finger on. A bag is constituted by its gradual distancing from a forbidden center, as if each part of it were dedicated to showing itself the most disinterested of all and obliging, with every backward step it takes, all the others to imitate it right away.

A bag, then, acts as a withdrawal, or, more accurately, as a form of asceticism, as fasting. Anyone who fasts wants to make a bag out of his interior. The dream of every faster is to turn into a balloon and disappear. A faster is a refugee, fleeing the gag of his bones and guts. Fleeing contact. A bag is just the same, a brief paean to the lack of contact, to floating up and away. In its interior everything lives in a state of hesitation and wobble, rocking from side to side, a slave to its mocking substance. Inside a bag, all is laughter and bad nerves.

A bag stops objects from falling, but unlike a table or a shelf, which halts things once and for all, a bag keeps halting them at every instant, since it can't fix them in place, can't offer any guarantees. Like a ship in mid-ocean, it goes along filled with objects that, by the grace of God, haven't fallen yet.

The objects are worth all the more, because, apparently, they're being protected from the dust on the ground, because they are survivors. Whatever floats, what's inside a bag, has, from moment to moment, just managed to keep itself at medium height, thanks to some miracle. Riches are a matter of balance and medium height. Rich folk are the ones who never need to reach up their arms in supplication or to bow down, offering their neck to the enemy, since they've got everything within reach, at medium height, in the bag, safe from the ground, saved from falling there. The rich have freed themselves from gravity; they are on the wind, the great s u r v i v o r s .

Wealth means floating but also cleansing. Moving around inside a bag, rubbing themselves against its lined walls, objects acquire a sheen. With its blackness and depth, a bag preserves the sheen of the things it contains and jostles around, for a bag is opaqueness *par excellence*. Its opaqueness derives directly from the dust that its outside picks up as it guards its contents against it. Yes, a bag is an ardent lifting, a tiring pilgrimage upwards, and arduous release in search of better air. Furthermore, a bag is opaque because it is a coral, a babbling babel of massed fingers, sensitive, compassionate, maternal and lusterless. But the fingers haven't renounced their claws; they've only pulled them in order to let them out suddenly at some later date. For that's how a bag operates, by postponement. Each segment temporarily relinquishes a part of its strength and does a little fasting, to make possible the final conjunction that ties them all into the same knot, the same pulse, in the shared undertaking that gives a bag its shape and meaning. This undertaking allows it its freedom from the ground; it is the spiritual adventure in which all parts join together as one. We might say: all the fingers reject an immediate hand for the sake of having one last Big Hand, one that activates all the circuits and showers blessings, like a heart whose slower beat reveals greater vigor and devotion, upon its grateful subordinates.

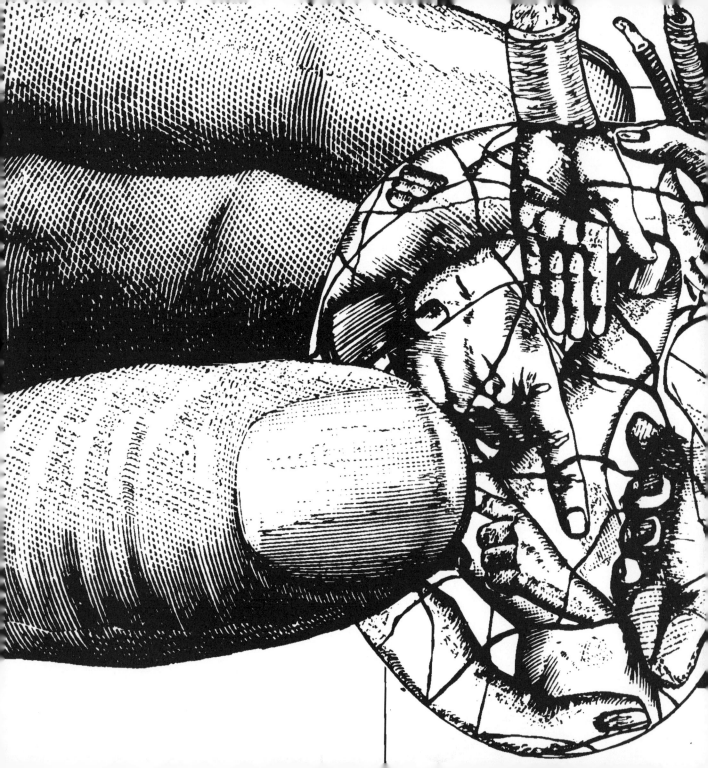

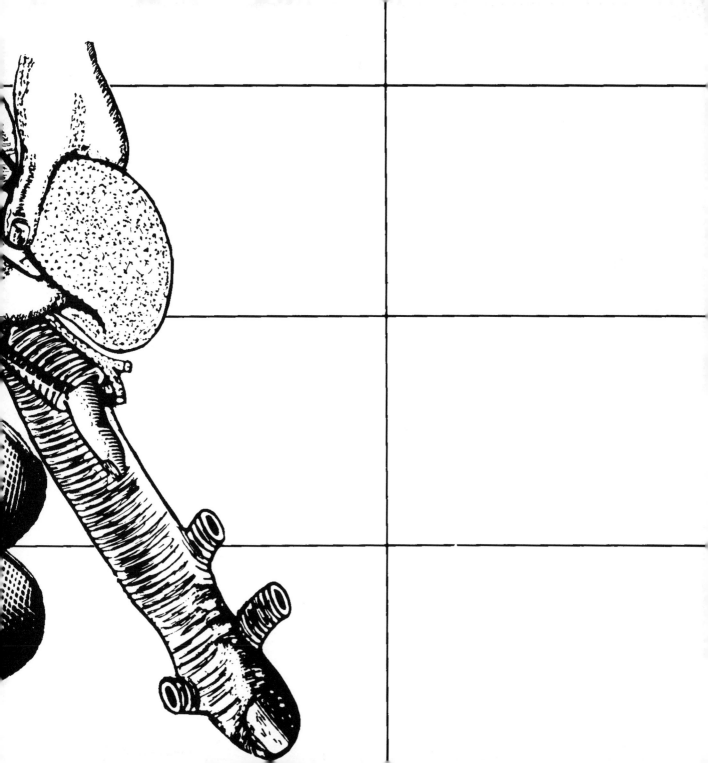

SCREW

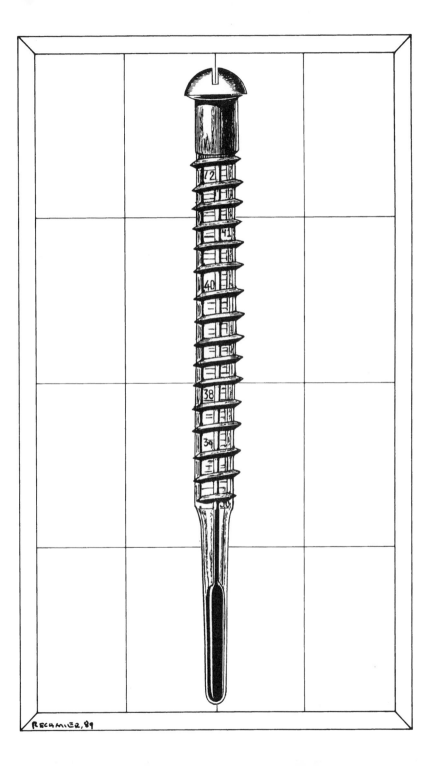

Oil is water equipped with hips, an impure sort of water that is on close terms with desire, time and death. Instead of advancing fluidly and unproblematically like water, oil insinuates itself and minces along. Where water, frank and anarchic, simpleminded and monotonous, liberates the world from its secrets, oil is a water that piles on secrets, water that lost its mission in some cranny and ever after forfeited its innocence. It is water with bad nerves. Exactly the same distinction exists between a nail and a screw. A screw is morose and circumspect, like oil. It is like a lubricated nail, manufactured to be mindful of other materials and to get along with them, careful not to impose its laws on them. In a screw the tough monologue of the nail has been transmuted into dialogue and negotiation. Hence the joints made by a screw are more durable. In place of a brusque conquest, there is piecemeal infiltration. The thing that a nail doesn't have a clue about, namely the action of grazing, reaches its highest temperature in a screw. As a result of a continual, uniform grazing action that resembles a smoldering fire, a screw lulls the material to rest, softening it up; it takes it without taking it, almost with disinterest, without appetite.

A nail is much more heroic and exciting. It moves in an epic world. A screw is ugly, torpid, asthmatic, short of initial impact, betraying no eagerness, no feeling whatever. But there lies its strength. How is it possible to resist something that never looks you full in the face but offers you only its perpetual profile? How can you argue with it? The threads of a screw are a profile in its purest form; they are simply the absence of all face and all intention. How can you tell when you see that spiral in motion whether it's going in or coming out? Whether it's addressing us or ignoring us? It's the great opportunist; it launches into a longwinded, winding discourse that doesn't allow us the slightest chance to interrupt it or to say no. There's no way into it. Rather than penetrate, it insinuates; it sneaks inside, totally impersonally, without showing its face. If it could, it would become invisible. Its strength resides in its longwindedness. As a talker, it is unbeatable. It's never lacking for an argument. It waits for its opportunity and then never shuts up. But the talkativeness of a screw relies more on suggestion and a wealth of examples than on the profundity of its reasoning. Reasons, like faces, are the children of pauses. A screw, which has never heard of a pause, is a superlative handler of examples. Each one of its turns is the equivalent of exclaiming "for example"; each turn of the screw is a different example of a nail, of the point that penetrates. A screw is a deluge of questions, but it never gives an answer. That's why, by sacrificing the excitement of entering its material with a blunt incisiveness, it secures every millimeter it gains as it advances. Like the delicate slime of a snail, it leaves behind, as it moves ahead, a winding track that guarantees it will find its way back cleanly, without obstacles.

And since its route is composed of questions, a hypothetical route in other words, a second screw can use it in the future. We can go as far as to say that one screw is always another, that it starts over at every turn, inexhaustible and replete with arguments. Hence it's careful never to go against the grain. It advances via the most timid of associations and the slenderest of similarities, without the slightest stumbling, like a hand that caresses us without ever detaching itself from our skin so that we don't awaken. Perhaps the spiral edges of a screw, in which continuity and rootedness, progression and permanence, have found a common solution, may shelter the mysterious secret of language. It's precisely this compromise solution, this innate caution in its conduct, that gives a screw its melancholic, almost tubercular appearance. It envies the impetus of a nail, its gleeful versatility, its Dionysian merriment, its uncompromised purity. By wanting to be a nail, a screw displays a yearning for a lost, pristine world where everything was transparent, effusive, ready to be discovered, obvious at first glance, where deals were violent but without subterfuge, without profiles, full in the face, with no sign of a frown, and where everything could be used as something else. That profound longing for a more fiery world is clearly visible in the head of a screw, a head always split painfully into two, like the face of frustration or a heart that's been deeply wounded.

SCISSORS

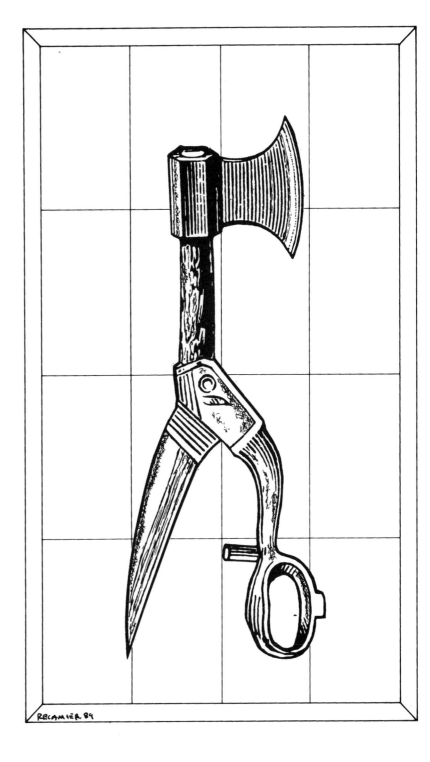

RECAMIER. 89

Scissors are ambassadors of cold. They bring us notice of the brilliant cruelties that cold is capable of when it's concentrated into a tool. While heat spreads out and fuses things together, concentrated cold does the opposite: it contracts and divides; it opens up gaps and reduces morale. Along with water, it possesses the power to reduce us, time after time, to the simplicity of ground-level existence and simultaneously to free us from the grubbiness of fruitless illusions. That's why we take baths, of course. Not merely to get cleaner. But to grow more realistic. The talk you get from scissors is always to the point. It can be summed up in the taunt: "There's no room here!" Between the steely blades of scissors, nothing can find room—apart from water, that is. Water's capable of unheard-of squirmings and can wriggle through the gap between the blades without taking the slightest drubbing. Everything else, however, has to back off, guilty of being either too fat or too slow. And if a thing doesn't choose to back off, it's forced to. That's what scissors do. Like a keel in seawater, they thrust things aside and clear a path for themselves. They work like a pair of hefty shoulders, easing others aside. Bit by bit they overthrow the opposition. They struggle body to body with one adversary, knock him over and go on to the next. As noiselessly as surgeons, they open a way through, not by demolishing but by leveling off, removing one foundation after another, subtracting supports. Scissors are specialists in deepening a crisis. They are creatures of evening. In the vertical, noonday light cast by a smooth surface, in a confrontation with the central expanse of an object, they're as useless as eunuchs. But let them slink to the edges of the object, to its twilit limits. Then by a series of sly maneuvers, by nipping the heads off the object's sentinels, they will manage to slide their way silently inward, undermining every defense. Undermining is a passion with them. They're cursed with a vindictive nature. And it's not hard to see why. Each blade of a pair of scissors loathes the other. They've been coerced into doing their dirty work together. Dirty, because we see no frontal attack, no heroic act of stabbing. Only an oblique act of slicing, undercover and chilling. In short, scissors behave like servile courtiers. Just as a forceful king summons his nobles to court and dominates them by making sure they rub each other the wrong way and whisper behind each other's backs, so these erstwhile daggers, once fervent-hearted and free-spirited until a sovereign screw forced them together, forfeit all their previous ardor in postures now decorous and docile. They grow courtly. They reek of courtliness, living under the sign of self-containment, suffocation and whispered gossip. While the underblade vilifies the object-victim, tracing out a thin line of death, the overblade comes down with a choking, chopping action. As the old trick has it, you toss a stone into the darkness, and when your imprudent enemy sticks his head out to see what's going on—whop! You chop it off with your sword. That's how scissors get ahead in this world, by surprising the opposition, outsmarting it. They attack the lumbar regions, the less sensitive parts. They begin with the youngest watchman, or the sleepiest, or the most isolated. Once they dispose of him, nothing can stop them. Yield them one single weak point, and they can find the rest for themselves. They are masters of deduction. They link one premise neatly to another and never for a second lose the

thread. They skip nothing. They move with mathematical
a   s   s   u   r   a   n   c   e   .
They live their lives wide-awake, almost on tiptoe, their
bitter eyes fixed on tomorrow. They resent the actual, the
present tenses of verbs, the surrounding landscape. They are
intoxicated with things subsequent. The word "tomorrow"
sums up their whole methodology. "Forward! Faster! Push
ahead!" squeaks the steel of their blades. "Into the future!
Tomorrow,   here   we   come!"
And yet, by means of two fingers and a glance, they allow
themselves to be manipulated, nicely, neatly, like elderly
spinsters, as if they weren't in direct contact with you but
were items of a venerable delicacy at the end of a dizzying
perspective of anterooms. Maybe that's why they won't
tolerate clumsy or inexpert handling the way other tools
will. They condone neither error nor fraud. In they go and
out they come. And that's that. They stay tense.
It's not uncommon to see children close one eye and study
the action of scissors, first opening the blades, then shutting
them. They want to discover which blade is the more
culpable, to unravel the mystery of scissors, to find their
center of gravity, the point of hesitation. Maybe they intuit
a secret softness in them, something like a heart that throbs
away under all that hardness, a seed, however tiny, of
self-surrender and extravagance. And, as usual, the kids are
on to something. Frequently, while scissors are immersed in
their work, while they're duly providing satisfaction, the
blades get along with each other famously. They keep a
date with heart, with art, with a genuine finesse. They
contract nickel-plated matrimony, each partner forgetful of
its lost bohemia. While they are opening up a careful path
through seas of cloth, of cardboard, of paper, suddenly they
discover that they're no longer playing tricks or sowing
seeds of calumny and terror, but are purely and simply
congratulating   one   another.

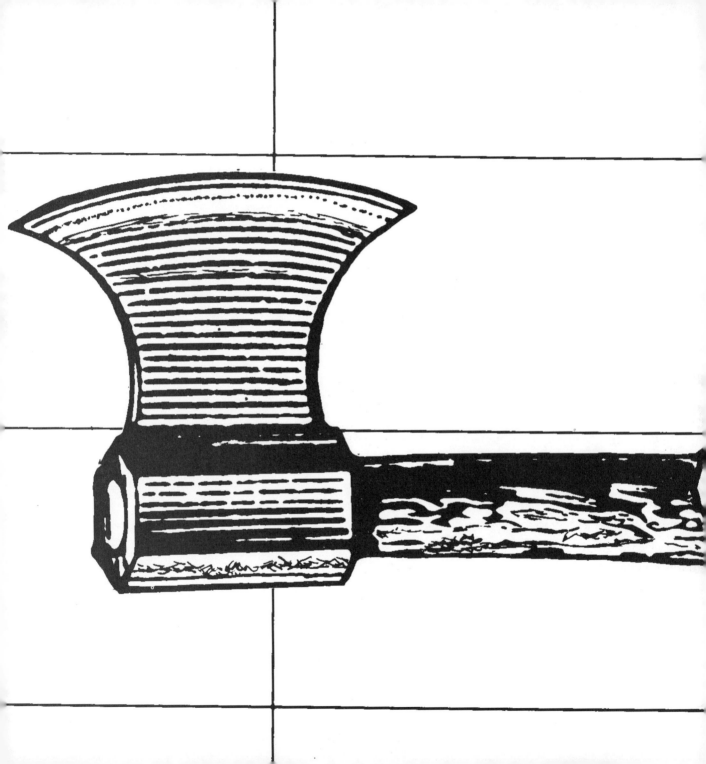

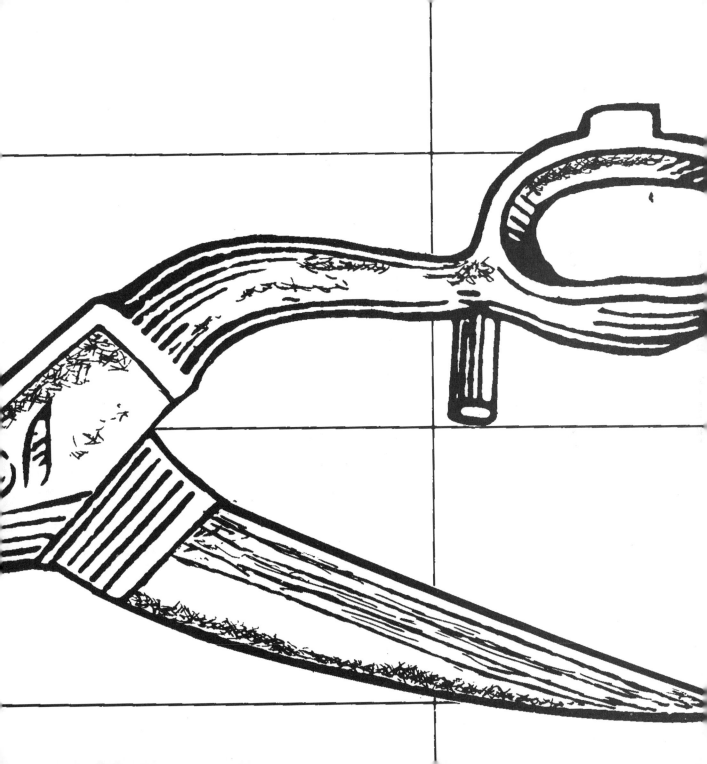

SPRING

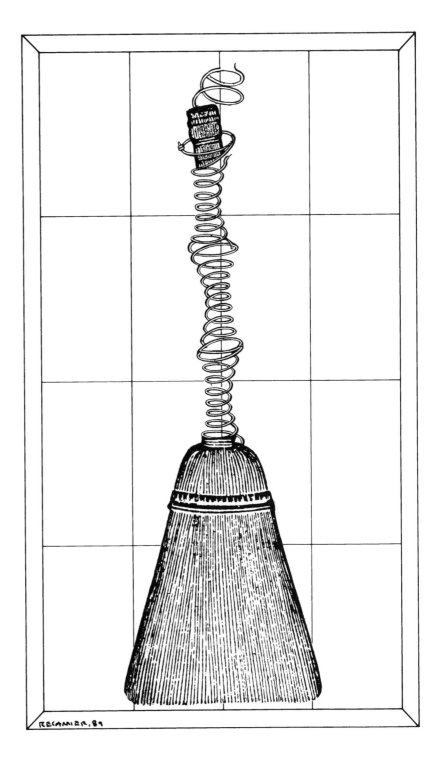

In a spring we discover a wire full of suspicion, a low-level flight within strict limits, one usually located in places like joints, enclosures and harsh encounters, where a good deal of patience and diplomacy is required. A spring is action in slow motion; it doesn't prevent contact but it breaks it into separate shots, turning it into an open-eyed encounter instead of a nerve-wracking collision. It is a branch of the lubricant family. Just like oil, it adds size to objects, as it were, creating around them a neutral zone which tempers their impact. To insert wires and springs into a mechanism is to bathe it in relativity, to give it a temperament that is determined by the quantity and distribution of the suspension—that is to say, by the intrinsic amounts of inventiveness and disconnectedness it has. Every spring is a velvety intermediary, a small abstraction, a cushion, a treaty, a lengthy, roundabout form of connection, and it's controlled by its family heritage, namely, the hushing-up of scandals; the siblings, cousins, uncles, aunts, in-laws and other relatives are linked together around us (or they should be) like a wall that protects us from inclement weather and allows us to confront bad times with a minimum of shock. Its parentage is a rung-like machine which brings moderation to the steepness of life by creating loops of relationships, hooks and grooves. It is a foe to slipping and s l i d i n g . In accordance with its nature, a spring distributes the force of an impact, making it mount a ladder, rung by rung, in order to attenuate or exhaust it. It works in many stages, by a succession of pockets, through endless antechambers. It suppresses the final meeting with the earth, that contact with the truth which we all share; it hides it continually, it postpones it, it comes up with a provisional grounding, with another fallacy, with one more antechamber, and the impulse peters out, like a duke asked to check out, coin by coin, pocket by pocket, the change left over from an errand performed by his servants. A spring dissuades. It is control at its purest. It leaves nothing to chance, it skips nothing, it channels and determines the dosage, it eliminates the miracle. The more spring you have, the less fire you get, or, rather, you get a fire that's more level-headed and restrained—in other words, a temperament. Wherever you find a spring, it lowers the volume and acclimatizes. Isn't every climate, in fact, an imperceptible balancing act, a barely audible humming of wires, a fever that cleanses and redraws our l i n e s ? Thus a spring is a healing and purifying agent. All healing, we could almost say, consists of a movement from concentration to distension, along a finely graduated slope. At the start of an illness, all our voices are confounded into one voice, in a single borderline. Then they go back to being separate and to losing themselves in the far distance. A tightly-knit clutch of earnest witnesses turns into vague, disconnected murmurings. That's what a cure, in great part, consists of: in suppressing, wherever they occur, the cadences of local vanities, in recalling the existence of those vaguer and more complex horizons that enclose us, in handing everything back to common and communal sense. A spring is a master in this art of generalization and the production of evidence. What it does by its movements is to snatch up an impulse and expose it, to lend it resonance, to grasp a particular truth and attach it to other truths, to entrust it to the common weal, although in the process it mediates it, giving it a paler cast—maybe just so that it can give it a paler cast. Like the art of rhetoric, which makes it possible to say anything, provided you level it off and file away its roughness, extracting the inflammatory bile, a spring resorts to strategy. Its shape is something it shares with every bridge. Is there anything more awesomely rhetorical than a bridge, anything less spontaneous or melodious? Every stone in a bridge, compared to the stones in any other edifice, is twice as cautious, doubly submissive, two times as worked over. Nothing excessive or inflammatory is allowed in a bridge. In the same way, there's only one way to make a spring— by mercilessly removing from a section of material, step by step, its brute nature, which is an inert and primitive thing, a solid single item. You don't leave it one ounce of its own native fire, you literally strip it of all its mystery, of every latent talent, correcting it with what has already been corrected, cleaning it up over and again until there's not the least doubt you have it in your total control, until there remains no trace of excitement or virginity in its condition. The spring was not invented; it was discovered when somebody decided, out of playfulness or necessity, to compress a bunch of stuff to its minimum, to clip its wings, to suppress its features, its sense of adventure. And there was the spring! Mutilated millimeter by millimeter, desiccated, almost at one short step from non-existence. That's why it's hard to manipulate it, to handle it. Once on the ground, it gives the impression of not really being on the ground, of not exerting any weight on the earth. It is the only tool that lacks style, for even something as simple as string or a hammer always has a minute irregularity, a hunchback or something that speaks to us of the thing's private temperature, of its own cast of mind. But a spring, no! It is stubbornly identical with itself, irreproachably so, stubbornly first in the class, stubbornly gold medal, stubbornly—why don't we say it, since it's on the tip of our t o n g u e s ? — h e l l i s h !

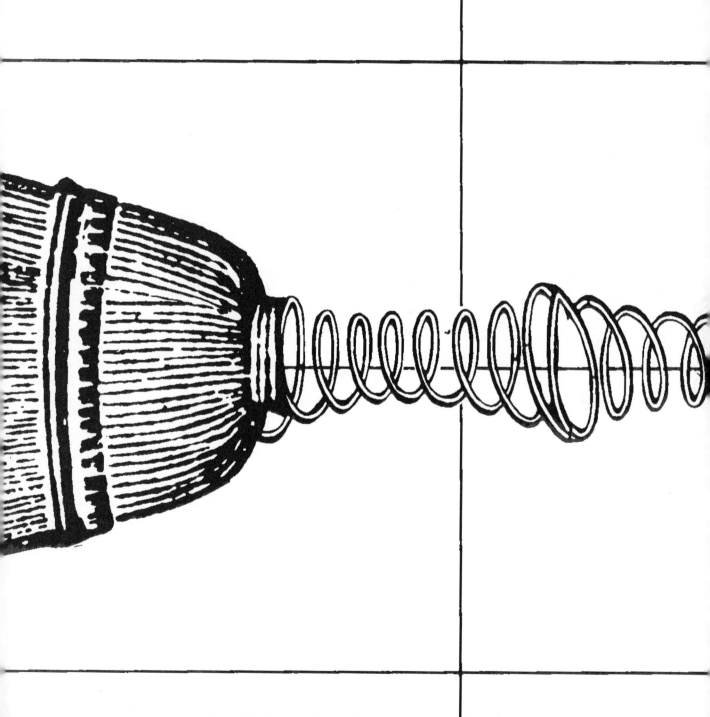

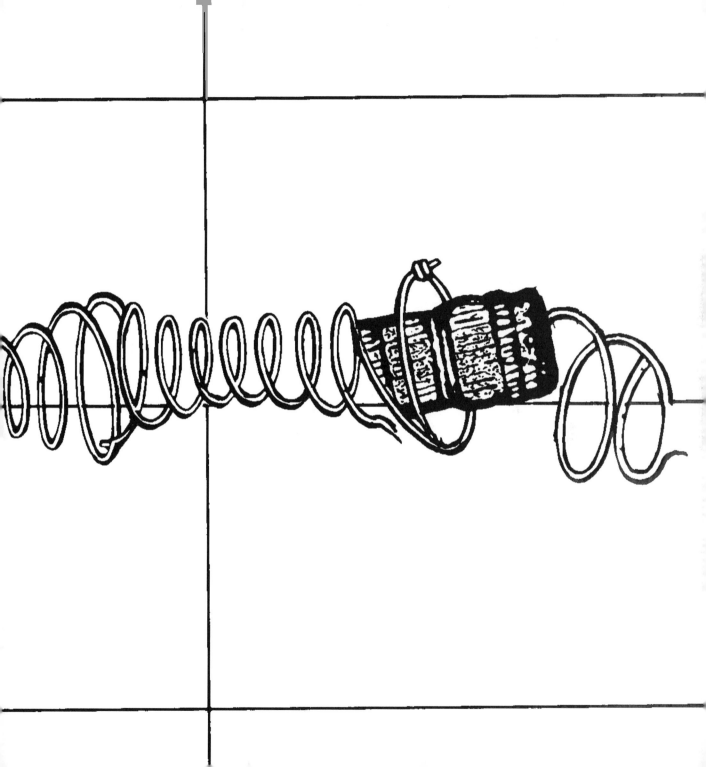

RAG

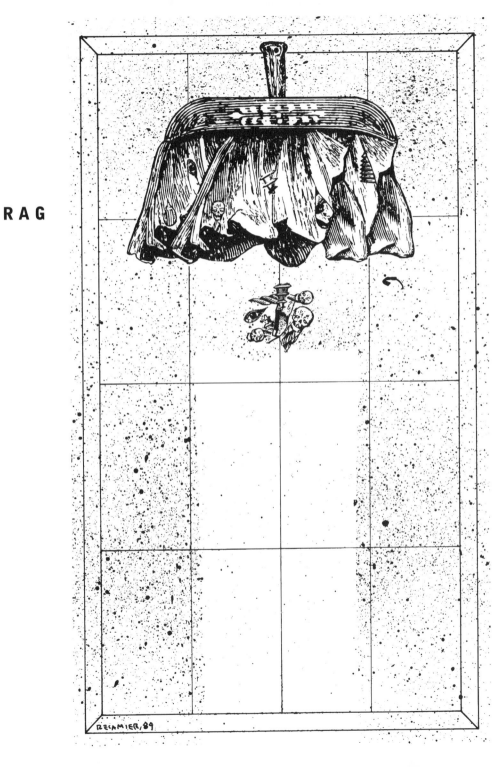

RECAMIER, 89

A rag also generalizes. There's no subtlety about it. Nothing like: Or so I thought, I was inclined to believe, at least they told me so, and there are two sides to every story. "To hell with it!" That's what a rag is forever shouting. "To hell with it!" It doesn't beat about the bush. Wipe it clean. Start a   f   r   e   s   h   . What would we do without rags? Our muck would stifle us. To save ourselves, we'd have to move on, dedicate ourselves to the nomadic life. But a rag helps stabilize our existence. It's a little breeze blowing through the home. Even today the gleam it leaves behind on the things it touches still carries a vestige of that pristine enchantment when people first settled down in community; silently and tirelessly it overcomes millennia of sloth and reconstructs that first day of days. Every act of wiping clean says, "Do you r   e   m   e   m   b   e   r   ?   " A rag works by absorption, chafing, collecting, pushing and simply seizing hold. Every act of wiping enhances the substantive and duly sets the adjectival in second place. A rag loves, venerates nouns. It is the guard dog of titles. Anything that is an attribute, an effect, an emanation or an epiphenomenon, it scornfully rejects as a waste of time. It scorns them as it scorns time itself, the thing it hates most. Every rag belongs to the school of Parmenides; it loves fixity of being, pure essentialness. If it could, every act of wiping would excavate a ditch around objects and leave them higher, more visible, more truly themselves. The passion of rags is to isolate, dispose of rubbish, leave things prouder than before; in short, to restore their names to t   h   e   m   . A rag has the power to astonish, to turn up out of nowhere. It is a stranger in the house, a messenger from its own world of obliging service that burdens itself with dust, the garbage of our world. But this world of rag is not another planet; it is fire; fire is always an alien world for us, far away, magical. A rag is the errand boy of fire; it is fire our hands can hold; it is one of the minor deities of the fiery pantheon.   It   is   applied   fire. Like fire, it works by means of enclosure, suffocation. It strips off the setting, cuts away neighborliness and connections, leaves things in a state of siege, high and dry, airless. It disbranches them from their family tree, reducing them to their own epitaphs. But in the process it underlines them with that back-and-forth movement it has. Like fire again, it places things in italics, without every creating anything else. Frankly, in the opinion of a rag, there's more stuff than enough already created, too much padding and waffling duplication. If it were left to rags, the world would be retrenched to a mere skeleton of itself, but a totally glamorous and unforgettable one, the world as one vast museum   of   gleaming   surfaces. A rag is in love with origins. Every act of wiping is an immersion in origins. And since origins are forever distancing themselves from us, the rag accepts the obligation to rub and rub, penetrating layer after layer to recover the original thing, the thing as it really is. Rags don't recognize the future; they make headway into the past. When we use a rag, we stop the world turning, we lean over our possessions, we bring them closer to fire, we once again fix them in place. "All you others, get out of here!" cries the rag. Isn't this the same secret cry that a spark makes when it unleashes fire, the same brutal indifference to others, the same violent act of introspection? Everything that covers up origins, that smears and daubs, releases the

heat in a rag. Once it gets going, it's a furious, pillaging brigand. It functions through rainclouds, a thousand orders soak it to the skin, it is a broth of imperatives. Imagine a large number of people stationed on a cliff edge. On a signal, they hurl themselves into the sea, one after another, each plunging on the heels of his neighbor into the same foamy area, like so many pebbles tossed by hand. That's the way a rag functions. Nothing stands fast, nothing steps back. It operates alarmingly, with a sudden, sunless whisk of the hand, going down the sides of
t   h   i   n   g   s   .
Without the concept of edge rags wouldn't exist. If surfaces continued endlessly, we could make do with brooms and pans. But they don't, so rags exist. Their arching movement, dangling and asthmatic, familiarizes itself with things truncated and cornered, and they know how to put to use that swarm of provincialisms and regional oddities. They take upon themselves concrete tasks, specific shines, local concerns. The rest is not their business; on edges and ledges they discharge their duties somewhat inconclusively. One could even say that since the things of this world possess corners and borders the rag never actually solves any problems; it merely postpones or delegates them to others. Hence that feeling of futility we get when we see somebody dusting or wiping down. We feel like screaming out: "The dust won't disappear, you know; it's only   getting   flung   around   a   bit." Still, when a rag has done its work, we do feel better. We feel that it's only right that everything wears away at the edges, provided that the surfaces around us have a nice bright gleam to them. We're such sentimentalists! Hence also our deep-down feeling that where the rag has been at

work the fire of that distant day, when houses first became homes, is once again refueled, burns brighter, bestows
c   o   m   f   o   r   t   .

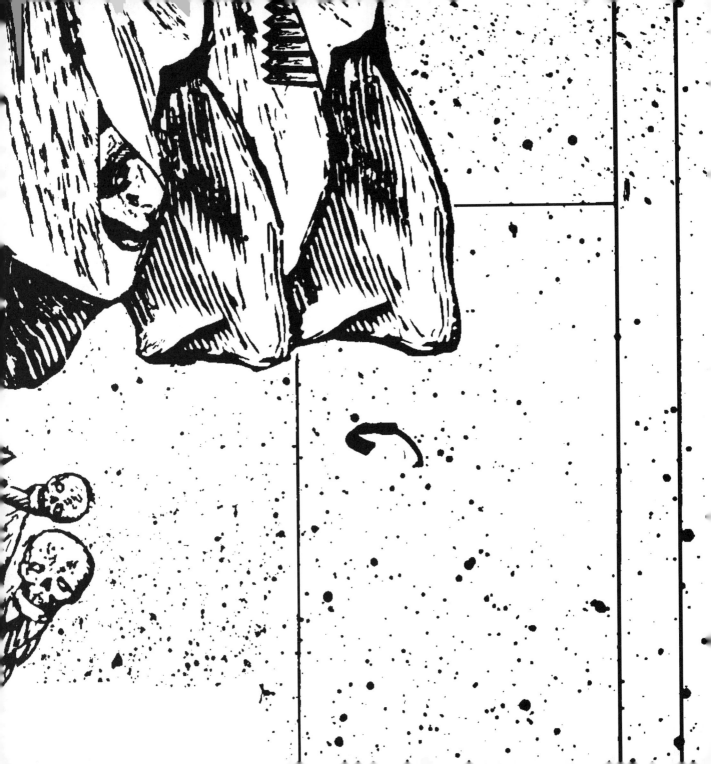

HAMMER

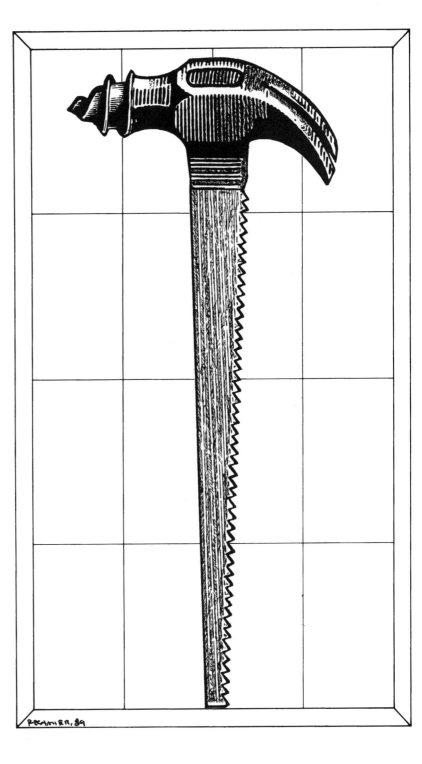

A hammer is at once the easiest of our tools and the most profound. No other tool fills the hand as much as a hammer does; none inspires the same degree of dedication to the job and such total acceptance of the task. With a hammer in hand, our body acquires its proper tension, a classic tension. Every statue ought to have a hammer, visible or invisible, like a second heart or a counterweight to offset the weight of the limbs. Wielding a hammer, we get rounded out, more integrated; it is exactly the one thing extra we need to feel ourselves permanent. Grasped by the hand, obtuse, cyclopean, childlike, with its weight and its feel, it gives us once again that sensation of freshness in a tool, of a satisfying extension to our bodies, of an effort directed without waste or frustration. O first-rate hammer! Willing brother! Few things are as straightforward as you! It acts like an epic poem; it's bilious, goatish and eagle-like. The force of a juicy anger has been attached to a wooden handle and has been left to ferment and toughen there. That's the way we get hammers—from a slow drip-drip of rage, which finally forms a scab at the end of the handle, an amalgam of wrath. Just shape that and polish it, and your hammer is ready to go. Passivity and power co-exist in a hammer. In fact, a hammer works by surprise, by nasty surprises, and its bruising strength is indebted not so much to its force as to its laconic delivery. It doesn't affirm, it skewers. All of a hammer's rage, slowly absorbed by the handle, slowly fermented, slowly assimilated, is expressed in one sharp bang! There's no time for anything else. A man who hammers, it would seem, combines in the hammer head the best of himself and his forefathers. The man himself, as a particular individual, is symbolized by the handle, which determines the willingness and direction of the blow, but the impact itself is entirely indebted to his past, a past heavy with the weight of the dead. A horde of the dead are packed into every hammer blow, your own dead, all that has been distilled in times before yours, everything tough that preceded you, and it's that toughness you hammer with, along with all your dead kin, whose purpose is to serve the living as a final hardness, as their sharpened steel, their armor plating. Anyone who tries to live without the dead, without a family tree, is barely alive and won't last long. Thus a hammer never says anything that hasn't been said before; no novel emotion ever changes its tone. The dead always produce the same response. Their productions get weaker with the passing of time, vast areas of memory crumble away, their vocabulary gets continually smaller until at last it is reduced to a single syllable, hard and o   b   d   u   r   a   t   e   . Upon reaching the kingdom of the dead, every dead person loses definition and his faltering voice is erased by the voices of others. Every hammer blow is like that, a flowing lava of voices that has been reduced to one sole syllable. Every hammer blow raises to the surface our lowest depths, which are often close to a petrified inertia, their connections with the here-and-now shrunk to a few dreams, a few pangs of conscience, a few blows from a hammer. That's why the hammer blows of one man are vastly different from those of another; they glue together parts that are peculiar to the individual, matters that defy translation. Maybe at some point, in the farthest distance, they do touch each other and mingle, but even so they retain

their separateness. Only the most sensitive of instruments could sort out those crude bangings into all their strata of voices that have been lost in the passage of time. But it would be a hellish instrument. We'd hear the warm of our dead speaking one by one, in a terrifying whirlwind of s   o   u   n   d   .
We have to bring the dead together and confuse them, to stop them frightening us, so that they'll let us live. We have to amalgamate them, squash them together, rub out their features and voices, until they linger on only as a choir, a far-distant   claypit,   a   half-shadow. That's the reason behind the invention of the hammer, its unified force. With a single blow it binds us to our dead and at the same time plunges them deep into the past. It buries them, gets them out from under our feet. When we talk to the dead through a hammer, we liberate ourselves from them. We can then go forward. The hammer flattens out, opens up a pathway, crushes down bumps in the road, levels off the track, heads toward tomorrow. A hammer is a prow,   no   more   no   less. But like every prow, it leaves behind a large wake, a choir of voices that are our dead kin, re-echoing in every blow. To move ahead is to move toward the dead. In every blow those who went before and those who are coming after, our yesterdays and our tomorrows, our liberty and our origins touch each other and fuse. In every blow we are nailed to the earth, redefined in a burst of bright flame, as if we were statues, not wholly alive, not wholly here, mildly classic and f   o   r   e   v   e   r   .

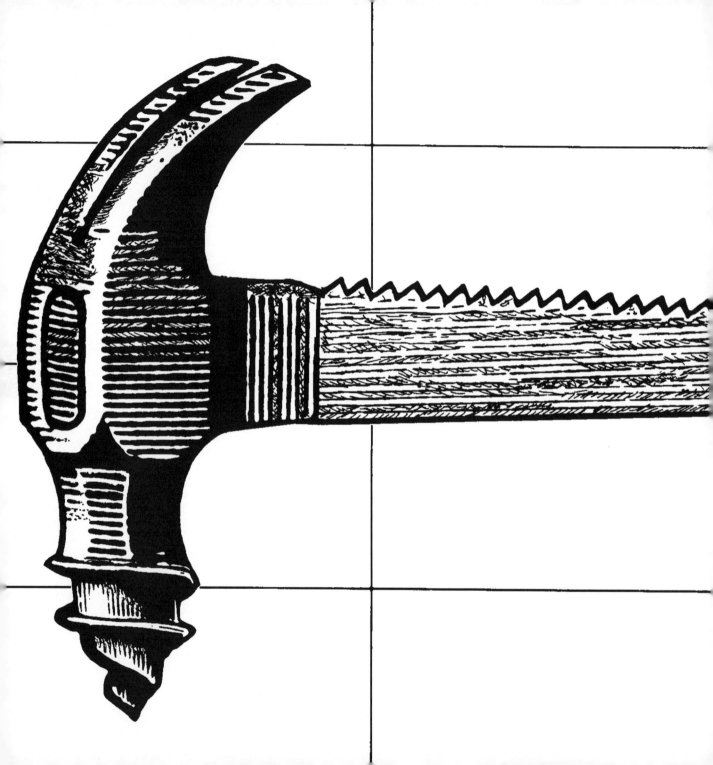

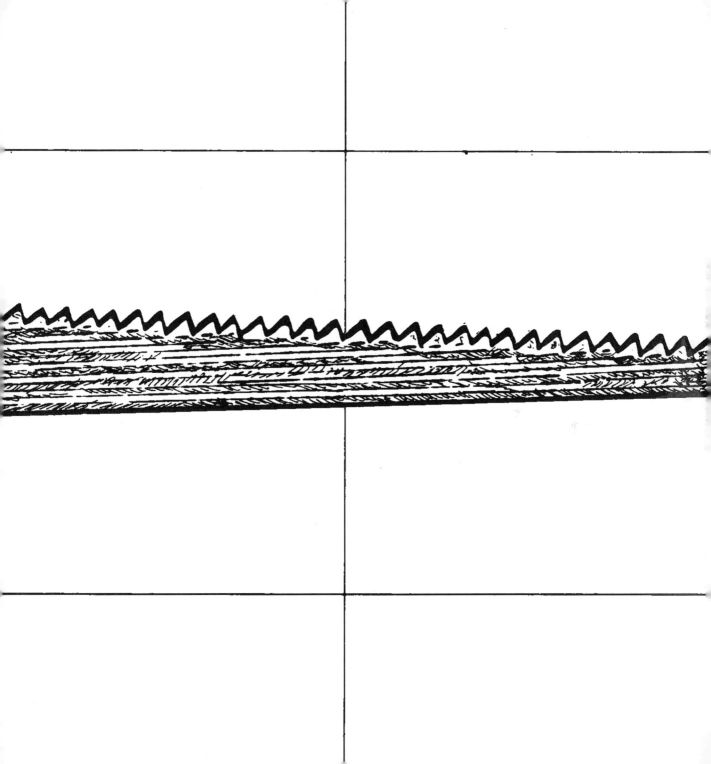

CONTRIBUTORS

FABIO MORÁBITO

was born in 1955 in Alexandria, Egypt, of Italian parents. He spent his childhood in Milan and in 1969 arrived with his family in Mexico. He writes all of his works in Spanish, his second language. His book of poems *Empty Lots (Lotes Baldios)* won the Carlos Pellicer Prize.

BERNARDO RECAMIER

is among the best known of Mexico's younger generation of graphic artists. His work adorns the covers of many of the country's most important magazines and cultural supplements.

GEOFF HARGREAVES, Ph.D.

was educated at the universities of Oxford, North Wales, and Victoria. He has taught in Spain and Mexico. He currently teaches at Frances Kelsey school in Mill Bay, British Columbia, Canada.